THE SCHOOL OF LIFE is dedicated to exploring life's big questions: *How can we fulfill our potential? Can work be inspiring? Why does community matter? Can relationships last a lifetime?* We don't have all the answers, but we will direct you towards a variety of useful ideas—from philosophy to literature, psychology to the visual arts—that are guaranteed to stimulate, provoke, nourish and console.

THESCHOOLOFLIFE.COM

By the same author:

The Art of Eloquence: Byron, Dickens, Tennyson, Joyce
Comedy: A Very Short Introduction
Lives of Victorian Literary Figures: Tennyson
Some Versions of Empson

Major works by Lord Byron:

Beppo
Childe Harold's Pilgrimage
Don Juan
Lara
Mazeppa
The Island
The Corsair
The Prisoner of Chillon
The Vision of Judgment

BYRON

Great Thinkers on Modern Life

Matthew Bevis

PEGASUS BOOKS
NEW YORK LONDON

BYRON

Pegasus Books LLC
80 Broad Street, 5th Floor
New York, NY 10004

ISBN: 978-1-60598-808-5

10 9 8 7 8 6 5 4 3 2 1

Printed in the United States of America
Distributed by W. W. Norton & Company, Inc.

It was such pleasure to behold him, such
   Enlargement of existence to partake
Nature with him
            (Byron, *Don Juan*, 1819–24)

CONTENTS

INTRODUCTION:
GOING TO SCHOOL
WITH BYRON

....

> Where did you learn all these secrets? I should like
> to go to school there.
>
> (Shelley, letter to Byron, 26 May 1820)

Shelley wrote this letter having just finished the first part of Byron's comic masterpiece, *Don Juan*. Byron obtained many of the secrets from what some might term 'the school of life'. This book is about what the poet learned there – and about what might be learned from him.

It should be conceded at the start that Byron is not convinced that you *can* get life lessons from books. '*Who* was ever altered by a poem?' he said. 'Reading or non-reading a book will never keep down a single petticoat.' More generally, he tends to distrust those who are keen to give advice, or those who claim to have the moral high ground (creatures he refers to as 'bigots of virtue'). After offering his own pearl of wisdom to a correspondent, the poet admitted that 'this is, like most good advice, impracticable'. Elsewhere he dwells on the example of Prometheus, the Titan who was punished for stealing fire from the gods:

> He teaches us the lesson taught so long,
> So oft, so vainly – learn to do no wrong!
>
> *(The Age of Bronze*, 1823)

'Even I', Byron admits, 'am just skilled to know the right and choose the wrong.' So a lesson, it would seem, is something that people can't – or won't – learn. But the poet doesn't always lament this state of affairs, and one of his finest qualities is his commitment to being incorrigible:

> Oh Pleasure! you're indeed a pleasant thing,
>   Although one must be damned for you, no doubt;
> I make a resolution every spring
>   Of reformation, ere the year run out,
> But, somehow, this my vestal vow takes wing,
>   Yet still, I trust, it may be kept throughout:
> I'm very sorry, very much ashamed,
> And mean, next winter, to be quite reclaimed.
>
> *(Don Juan*, 1819–24)

Not that ashamed, we suspect. Besides, next winter is a long way off. What Byron really reclaims is a relishing of present experience. As he puts it elsewhere, he wants to 'learn experience', which is not necessarily the same thing as learning *from* it.

Having said all this, Byron does assert in *Don Juan* that his poem is a 'great moral lesson', and he noted to a friend that 'it is my respect for morals that makes me so indignant against its vile substitute: cant'. He's often insistent that poetry should try 'to make man better and wiser', and he praised his literary hero, Alexander Pope, for writing 'Ethical poetry, in my mind the highest of all poetry'. Pope's verse, he said, was 'the Book of Life', and Byron was an ardent defender of the idea that books should take their bearings from everyday experience: 'Almost all of Don Juan is *real* life – either my own – or from people I knew.' Despite his scepticism about what writing could achieve, he explained that he wrote 'as a *means* to obtain influence over men's minds – which is a power in itself and in its consequences'. In the chapters that follow, I'll be exploring some of the ways in which that power might be conceived and put to use.

To go to school with Byron is not to go to Sunday school. In *Don Juan*, the prim and proper Donna Inez 'sets up a Sunday school'

> For naughty children, who would rather play
> (Like truant rogues) the devil, or the fool.
>   (*Don Juan*, 1819–24)

The poet, though, is enamoured of truant rogues – and of the special ways in which they learn things. Later in the poem, Juan and Haidee fall for each other as she tries to teach him her language. This is how life lessons are learned in Byron's universe:

> And now, by dint of fingers and of eyes,
>   And words repeated after her, he took
> A lesson in her tongue; but by surmise,
>   No doubt, less of her language than her look:
> As he who studies fervently the skies
>   Turns oftener to the stars than to his book,
> Thus Juan learned his alpha beta better
> From Haidee's glance than any graven letter.
>
> 'Tis pleasing to be schooled in a strange tongue
>   By female lips and eyes – that is, I mean,
> When both the teacher and the taught are young,
>   As was the case, at least, where I have been;
> They smile so when one's right, and when one's wrong
>   They smile still more, and then there intervene
> Pressure of hands, perhaps even a chaste kiss; –
> I learned the little that I know by this.
>
>   (*Don Juan*, 1819–24)

It's not so much *what* such charismatic, seductive teachers communicate, but *how* they do it (a 'glance', a 'look', a 'smile'). This is Byron's kind of teaching (he was always averse to 'the drilled dull lesson, forced down word by word'). We learn his lessons not by rote, but rather take them 'by surmise'. And in Byronic schooling, the teacher and the taught are partners in crime, part of a double act in which it's not entirely clear who has the upper hand. Perhaps this book might be better called *Life Lessons in Byron*, rather than *from Byron*. For this poet, a lesson isn't something that is handed down. It's more like a language you can learn, a mode of being and speaking in the world: 'he took / A lesson in her tongue'. To speak Byron is to put yourself to school in unpredictable ways. A new language, he suggests, can provide a new repertoire for living.

*

Singular . . . most curious . . . nauseating, perhaps, but how quite inexpressibly significant.
　　(Henry James, on reading Byron's private papers)

Everyone thinks they know Byron. And they know that to know him is a kind of risk. Lady Caroline Lamb's description – 'he's mad, bad, and dangerous to know' – has stuck. He's the Romantic wild-child who can't be tamed. 'I was born for opposition,' he proclaimed. But on other occasions he was less strident: 'If you hear ill of me', he wrote to one correspondent, 'it is probably not untrue though perhaps exaggerated.' There is a lot that is not untrue about Byron. He was famous for being infamous, and tales of sodomy and scandal, incest and intrigue, were never very far away. Here was a poet who was intent on being more than a poet. 'I do not draw well with Literary men,' he confessed. 'I never know what to say to them after I have praised their last publication.' In *Beppo* he added: 'One hates an author that's *all author.*' And so this author had many other lives to live: the parliamentary speaker, the Regency rake, the European voyager, the defender of Greek liberty, and so on. Wherever people looked, the man was up to something. T. S. Eliot was right: 'Byron has the cardinal virtue of never being dull.'

He was born in 1788, a year before the French Revolution broke out. 'My whole life was a contest,' he said, and early on it looked as though political contests would claim his attention. He took his seat in the House of Lords in 1809, making speeches in favour of Catholic Emancipation and other liberal causes. After a Grand Tour of the Iberian peninsula and the Turkish dominions in the Levant, he published the first part of *Childe Harold's Pilgrimage* in 1812. It was an overnight success: 'I awoke one morning and found myself famous.' Later, he boasted:

I was reckoned a considerable time
The grand Napoleon of the realms of rhyme.
(*Don Juan*, 1819–24)

Certainly, the influence of the man – or the myth of the man – across Europe was staggering; *Don Juan* was the bestselling work of the Romantic period, and was read by more people in the first twenty years after publication than any previous work of English literature. Annabella Milbanke, whom the poet married in 1815 and separated from less than a year later, was one of many caught up in what she termed 'Byromania'.

The poet left England in 1816 and never returned. He stayed with the Shelley circle at Lake Geneva, before moving on to settle (although 'settle' is never quite the right word for Byron) in Italy. After a string of dangerous liaisons and flings, he fell in love with Teresa Guiccioli in 1819. Signing off one letter to her, he wrote: 'I kiss you more than I have ever kissed you – and this (if Memory does not deceive me) should be a fine number, counting from the beginning.' Byron set sail for Greece in 1823, and he died there a few months later whilst supporting the Greeks in their fight for independence.

That's the briefest of sketches of Byron's life. I'll occasionally draw on biographical details in the chapters that follow, although it seems to me that myth and mania have often obscured what's really interesting about Byron as a writer and thinker. This book shares a little of Dante Gabriel Rossetti's impatience with the poet's biographers – as Rossetti put it: 'If Byron fucked his sister he fucked her and there an end.' The poet's life may inform his writing, but his writing also allowed him to reinvent his life, and we need to go beyond the scandal and the headlines in order to learn something from him. I want to focus on Byron's genius for talking and thinking on paper.

In an interview in 2009, Bob Dylan was asked: 'What kind of artist are you?' 'I'm not sure, Byronesque maybe,' he replied. It's a good answer, partly because to be a Byronesque person or artist (maybe) is itself to be unsure of who you are. Byron is Byronesque, or Byronish – which is not the same thing as being a proponent of Byronism, or hedonism, or optimism, or pessimism, or – in the poet's words – 'some other hard name ending in "*ism*"'. He teaches, but he teaches by stealth and indirection, by not always saying the thing we might expect him to say. 'There is pleasure in the pathless woods,' he writes delectably in one poem, and he certainly likes those woods, yet it's interesting to find the notoriously pleasure-seeking poet also claiming that 'the more intellectual our pleasure, the better for the pleasure – and for us too'. This book is about the ways in which we might have better pleasure.

1

HOW TO BECOME YOURSELF

....

> May I add a few words on a subject on which all
> men are supposed to be fluent, and none agreeable,
> – Self?
>> (Byron, 'Dedicatory Epistle to Thomas Moore',
>> *The Corsair*, 1814)

Wherever Byron went, he found that his reputation preceded him. The poet said of 'Ambition', 'Love', and 'Fame':

> they came unsought, and with me grew,
> And made me all which they can make – a name.
>> ('Epistle to Augusta', 1816)

To get away from being a name was one of the reasons Byron left England. From Italy, he wrote:

> I am a nameless sort of person,
> (A broken Dandy lately on my travels)
>> (*Beppo*, 1818)

What might one gain by becoming a nameless sort of person? The Dandy's predicament is of course a special case (nobody's quite as famous as Byron), but many of us have felt beholden to a version of ourselves that we've grown uncomfortable with, or at least felt that our personality is a bit of a drag:

> My very chains and I grew friends,
> So much a long communion tends
> To make us what we are
>
> *(The Prisoner of Chillon*, 1816)

We are often chained to work (so many first encounters seem to open with the question: 'What do you do?') and we are even chained to play (the next question is often: 'What do you do, then, when you're *not* working?') Like a long commute, a 'long communion' with the habitual can whittle down a life to a mere lifestyle.

Byron tempts us to remake what we are. The philosopher Stanley Cavell has suggested that 'ignorance of myself is something I must work at', and Byron encourages this kind of unpredictable work – he confessed to Lady Blessington that 'if I know myself, I should say that I have no character at all'. 'And yet – and yet – always *yet* and *but*,' he writes in his journal. Being himself always led to a *yet* and a *but*:

> Temperate I am – yet never had a temper;
>   Modest I am – yet with some slight assurance;
> Changeable too – yet somehow *Idem semper:*
>   Patient – but not enamoured of endurance;
> Cheerful – but, sometimes, rather apt to whimper:
>   Mild – but at times a sort of *Hercules furens:*
> So that I almost think that the same skin
> For one without – has two or three within.
>
> (*Don Juan*, 1819–24)

It's tricky to pin the 'I' to a consistent position; it seems he can't even 'think' what he says, he can only 'almost think' it. Byron's confession asks us to consider whether any of us are ever quite equal to ourselves – and whether we really want to be. Can we find ways to avoid feeling exasperated – or even just plain bored – by what we are? To become ourselves, how might we commit to the adventure of becoming new to ourselves?

It's worth noting at the outset just how much of everyday life is given over to thinking about unlived lives. The poet would have agreed with Oscar Wilde: 'One's real life is so often the life that one does not lead.' This is why Byron was a writer: 'To withdraw *myself* from *myself* (oh that cursed selfishness!) has ever been my sole, my entire, my sincere motive in scribbling at all.' Why write? Or daydream? Or fantasize? Byron replies:

11

'Tis to create, and in creating live
A being more intense, that we endow
With form our fancy, gaining as we give
The life we image, even as I do now.
What am I? Nothing; but not so art thou,
Soul of my thought! with whom I traverse earth,
Invisible but gazing, as I glow
Mixed with thy spirit, blended with thy birth,
And feeling still with thee in my crushed feeling's
dearth.

(Childe Harold's Pilgrimage, 1812–18)

So something can be made out of 'Nothing'. Rather than trying to improve ourselves, perhaps we could aim to invent ourselves. To imagine a self can be to create one:

The beings of the mind are not clay;
Essentially immortal, they create
And multiply in us a brighter ray
And more beloved existence: that which Fate
Prohibits to dull life, in this our state
Of mortal bondage, by these spirits supplied
First exiles, then replaces what we hate;
Watering the heart whose early flowers have died,
And with a fresher growth replenishing the void.

(Childe Harold's Pilgrimage, 1812–18)

The first passage spoke of a 'being' and a 'spirit', this one of 'beings' and 'spirits'. Putting things into the plural suggests that to become ourselves we need to stop seeing selfhood as a kind of essence, and to think of it as more like a series of performances – not something we are, but something we do. Byron half-became Childe Harold, and readers might follow his lead. As Freud noted: 'Only in the realm of fiction do we find the plurality of lives which we need.' To write – and to read – is to go forth and multiply.

The realm of fiction offers lessons for living because fiction *is* living. Armed with this knowledge, you can generate a space in which to become newly serious by playing around a little. In *The Vision of Judgment*, Byron focuses on the author who, in order to attack the repressive policies of George III, wrote under the pseudonym of 'Junius':

The moment that you had pronounced him one,
    Presto! his face changed, and he was another;
And when the change was hardly well put on,
    It varied, till I don't think his own mother
(If that he had a mother) would her son
    Have known, he shifted so from one t'other,
Till guessing from a pleasure grew a task,
At this epistolary 'iron mask' . . .

I've an hypothesis – 'tis quite my own;
    I never let it out till now, for fear
Of doing people harm about the throne,
    And injuring some minister or peer
On whom the stigma might perhaps be blown;
    It is – my gentle public, lend thine ear!
'Tis, that what Junius we are wont to call,
Was *really, truly*, nobody at all.

                              (*The Vision of Judgment*, 1822)

This could mean that 'Junius' was more than one person, or that the writer behind the pseudonym didn't resemble the published persona. Or maybe it means that whatever 'we are wont to call' a person, whenever we 'pronounce him one', we miss the point. To recall the Arctic Monkeys' riff on a line from Alan Sillitoe's novel: 'Whatever people say I am, that's what I'm not.' We're so often possessed by the idea of people having a self – and dictated to by the imperative: 'Just be yourself' – that we perhaps neglect to ask: Are we ever really in possession of a self? Is it even the sort of thing you can own?

Byron prompts us to entertain the idea that a self might be a kind of relationship or a contract. 'To know who I am', the philosopher Charles Taylor writes, 'is a species of knowing where I stand.' You can't be a self in solitary confinement, and you can't keep standing still. As Byron writes:

The heart is like the sky, a part of heaven,
But changes night and day too, like the sky.

(*Don Juan*, 1819–24)

The poet's hope is that, by embracing the unknow-ability of who we are, we might discover new ways of enjoying ourselves and other people. This is why forms of carnival and masquerade are so important to him:

I hate inconstancy – I loathe, detest,
    Abhor, condemn, abjure the mortal made
Of such quicksilver clay that in his breast
    No permanent foundation can be laid;
Love, constant love, has been my constant guest,
    And yet last night, being at a masquerade,
I saw the prettiest creature, fresh from Milan,
Which gave me some sensations like a villain.

But soon Philosophy came to my aid,
    And whispered, 'think of every sacred tie!'
'I will, my dear Philosophy!' I said,
    'But then her teeth, and then, Oh heaven! her eye!
I'll just inquire if she be wife or maid,
    Or neither – out of curiosity.'
'Stop!' cried Philosophy, with air so Grecian,
(Though she was masqued then as a fair Venetian).

(*Don Juan*, 1819–24)

So it's not just the 'I' who is inconstant, but 'Philosophy'
herself, who beguilingly turns from a personification
into a person. And to turn into a person is always to
turn into something of a mystery (note that Philosophy
was masqued 'then', which means she might be other
things at other times). She flirts with our narrator just as
our narrator flirts with us. Byron is perpetually encouraging us to flirt because flirtation is itself a pleasing
disorientation of selves, an acceptance of ambiguity. As
the poet wrote elsewhere about the carnival:

> all ranks are jostled – and mingled – and delighted
> – and all this without fear – observance – or offence
> . . . Curiosity is always excited – some times Passion
> – and occasionally Pleasure. –– If you do not always
> recognize you are generally recognized . . . and the
> jest – or the hint – or the present of a flower with
> which you are greeted have a novelty even from a
> former acquaintance. –– Life becomes for a moment
> a drama without the fiction.
>
> ('An Italian Carnival', 1823)

Although it may only last 'for a moment', the carnival
is a gift to take back to everyday life. It's a reminder
that novelty can be found in the seemingly familiar, and
that to remain strange to each other can be a pleasure
as well as a predicament. To learn to *become yourself*,
you might embrace the double meaning in the phrase

(as when you offer compliments like 'that outfit really becomes you'). How do I look with this self on? Does it become me?

Reading Byron, it's hard not to be seduced by the dashing nature of his re-descriptions; what people call 'inconstancy', for example, is really a 'sort of adoration of the real'. Yet *Don Juan* also gestures towards another kind of wisdom. Here the protagonist is entranced by the spellbinding Lady Adeline, but he's also wary, for he begins to entertain 'Some doubt how much of Adeline was *real*':

> So well she acted, all and every part
>   By turns – with that vivacious versatility,
> Which many people take for want of heart.
>   They err – 'tis merely what is called mobility,
> A thing of temperament and not of art,
>   Though seeming so, from its supposed facility;
> And false – though true; for surely they're sincerest,
> Who are strongly acted on by what is nearest.
>
> *(Don Juan*, 1819–24)

So is 'mobility' a good or a bad thing? 'For *surely* they're sincerest' sounds like special pleading, yet Byron clearly wants readers to appreciate the value of the 'versatility' too. His note to the stanza compounds the uncertainty:

> In French, 'mobilité' ... It may be defined as an
> excessive susceptibility of immediate impressions
> – at the same time without *losing* the past; and is,
> though apparently useful to the possessor, a most
> painful and unhappy attribute.
>
> (*Don Juan*, 1819–24)

Thomas Moore said that Byron 'was fully aware not only of the abundance of this quality in his own nature, but of the danger in which it placed consistency and singleness of character'. The poet confessed as much: 'I could not resist the *first* night of any thing.' What 'mobility' initially seems to offer us is a vision of our lives (and our selves) as a series of great first nights. Yet that's not necessarily going to get us through the morning after, which is perhaps why Byron adds the rider: 'at the same time without *losing* the past'. There's no simple way of avoiding the difficulties that this contradiction entails, a contradiction between a mobile, self-becoming inclination for 'what is nearest', and a need for a past (and a future) we can rely on. Still, the sheer appetite Byron has for describing difficulties somehow makes them easier to bear:

> If people contradict themselves, can I
>   Help contradicting them, and every body,
> Even my veracious self? – But that's a lie;
>   I never did so, never will – how should I?

He who doubts all things, nothing can deny;
   Truth's fountains may be clear – her streams are
      muddy,
And cut through such canals of contradiction,
That she must often navigate o'er fiction.
                                        (*Don Juan*, 1819–24)

Navigation: this is what the poet can help us with. Yet, as literary theorist and philosopher Roland Barthes observed, 'anyone who speaks about himself gets lost', and Byron certainly encourages readers to get lost too. To become ourselves, then, is to keep some sense of bearings or direction, yet also to make ourselves up as we go along. We need to wake up each morning enquiring not just: 'What will the day bring me?' but also: 'Which *me* shall I bring to the day?' It's a tricky balancing act between expectation and improvisation, and it might be suspected that the poet is not inclined to give us entirely consistent pieces of advice. But then, as he notes elsewhere:

   if a writer should be quite consistent,
How could he possibly show things existent?
                                        (*Don Juan*, 1819–24)

2

HOW TO THINK
WITH YOUR BODY

....

> In coming out, one night, from a ball, with Mr Rogers,
> as they were on their way to their carriage, one of the
> link-boys ran on before Lord Byron, crying, 'This way,
> my Lord.' 'He seems to know you,' said Mr Rogers.
> 'Know me!' answered Lord Byron, with some degree
> of bitterness in his tone – 'everyone knows me, – I
> am deformed.'
>
> > (Thomas Moore, *The Works of Lord Byron*
> > *with his Letters and Journals*, 1833)

The poet Arthur Symons had two complaints about
Byron: 'He never forgets that he is a lord, and that one
of his feet is not perfect.' But the poet was never *allowed*
to forget the club foot he was born with, as he observed
to his publisher:

> I see all the papers in a sad commotion ... the
> Morning Post in particular has found out that I am a
> sort of Richard 3rd – deformed in mind & *body* – the

His mother saw his foot as the mark of the devil, something akin to a cloven hoof. (As Arnold recalls of his
mother in Byron's play *The Deformed Transformed*:
'She beheld my shape was hopeless.') Reviewers of
his poetry spoke later of 'the deformity of vice'. One
critic suggested that 'Byron's lameness was to blame'
for his poetry's 'immorality', and the poet frequently
commented on the links between his writing and his
body, saying wryly of one of his works that it was 'scrib-
bled "stans pede in uno" [standing on one foot] – the
only foot I have to stand on'.

Byron's feelings of instability might be seen as an
extreme case, but many of us worry about body image
– or about what our bodies are meant to say about us.
S, M, L or XL – what's the right size for a human being?
Byron claimed that the ideal poet

'Every body' – two words, not one – is saying two things
at once: 'everybody has feelings', and 'everyone's

body is able to feel through the senses'. This blending of cerebral and corporeal perspectives provokes a series of questions: Can 'good sense' be fostered by attention to our senses? What, exactly, do our bodies know? And what could be gained by thinking *with* as well as *about* them?

The first thing Byron draws attention to is how our ideals can demonize our bodies. Having run through a list of loves ('Platonic love', 'love of God', 'the love of Sentiment'), he adds:

> Besides all these pretences
> To love, there are those things which words name
>   Senses: –
>
> Those movements, those improvements in our bodies
>   Which make all bodies anxious to get out
> Of their own sand-pits to mix with a Goddess,
>   For such all Women are at first no doubt.
> How beautiful that moment! and how odd is
>   That fever which precedes the languid rout
> Of our Sensations! What a curious way
> The whole thing is of clothing souls in clay!
> *(Don Juan*, 1819–24)

Only Byron could put 'sand-pits' and 'Goddess' in the same line and still make the line sing. Everybody – or rather, every body – should get out more. Movement

23

is an improvement. One of the great pleasures of reading Byron is the appetite he has – and gives – for the languid rout of sensation. Writing like this refuses to be ashamed or critical of anyone's body.

Don Juan invites us to see thought itself as a kind of bodily sensation. Byron's headmaster said he had a 'mind that feels', and the poet described Juan as 'he whose very body was all Mind'. Others, too, keep the body in mind. Here's the moment Haidee first sets eyes on Juan when he's just been washed up on shore:

And walking out upon the beach, below
    The cliff, towards sunset, on that day she found,
Insensible, — not dead, but nearly so, —
    Don Juan, almost famished, and half drowned;
But being naked, she was shocked, you know,
    Yet deemed herself in common pity bound,
As far as in her lay, 'to take him in,
A stranger' dying, with so white a skin.

                        (*Don Juan*, 1819–24)

'She was shocked, you know.' The maiden could be shocked because she's scandalized by Juan's nakedness. But maybe she feels shocked because she feels curious – feels shocked, in fact, *by* her curiosity, a curiosity that is itself already warm with desire. Where, the poem gently enquires, does Haidee's pity end and her passion begin? Somewhere around Juan's midriff, perhaps.

Byron's aside – 'you know' – is a reminder of how our own thoughts often provide a cover story for what our bodies are really up to, and the poet's wordplay becomes a means to signal how our verbal expressions, like our minds, are inflected by body matters. When, for example, we learn that Haidee intends 'to take him in', we might wonder whether she means to play more than the Good Samaritan. The words we think with are haunted by the body's ubiquitous presence and its need to orient itself: people are denigrated as *crooked* or *twisted*, or praised for being *upright* or *upstanding*; affection is *warmth*; happy is *up*; sad is *down*; help is *support*; difficulties are *burdens*; and so on. Emotions – as the word suggests – are housed in movement. In *Don Juan*, Byron often hints at how physiology shapes thought ('Indigestion', he notes, 'perplexes / Our soarings with another sort of question'), and at how our thoughts and feelings feed back to the body (lovesickness is 'nausea, or a pain / About the lower region of the bowels').

Spending time with thoughts like these can help us to stay balanced by encouraging us to remain conversant with how different sides of ourselves interact. Here's Juan – caught between 'soarings' and 'lower regions':

He thought about himself, and the whole earth,
    Of man the wonderful, and of the stars,
And how the deuce they ever could have birth;
    And then he thought of earthquakes, and of wars,

> How many miles the moon might have in girth,
>   Of air-balloons, and of the many bars
> To perfect knowledge of the boundless skies;
> And then he thought of Donna Julia's eyes.
>
> In thoughts like these true wisdom may discern
>   Longings sublime, and aspirations high,
> Which some are born with, but the most part learn
>   To plague themselves withal, they know not why:
> 'Twas strange that one so young should thus concern
>   His brain about the action of the sky;
> If *you* think 'twas philosophy that this did,
> I can't help thinking puberty assisted.
>
> (Don Juan, 1819–24)

To describe the seat of Juan's thoughts as his 'brain' (rather than, say, his mind) is to accentuate the physicality of his most sublime moments. Yet Byron is not really mocking Juan here: the young man 'thought' one thing, '*you* think' another, and the poet 'can't help thinking' yet another, but we're all thinking with our bodies. The philosopher David Hume suggested that 'all probable reasoning is nothing but a species of sensation. 'Tis not only in poetry and music, we must follow our taste and sentiment, but likewise in philosophy.' One of the things Byron teaches is that, if we wish to become truly philosophical about everyday life, we cannot wholly escape the physical – even though

we may wish to avoid reducing things *to* the physical. In fact, the first use of the word 'physique' in our
language, according to the *Oxford English Dictionary*, is
credited to Byron:

What an antithetical mind! – tenderness, roughness
– delicacy, coarseness – sentiment, sensuality –
soaring and grovelling, dirt and deity – all mixed up
in that one compound of inspired clay!

It seems strange; a true voluptuary will never
abandon his mind to the grossness of reality. It is by
exalting the earthly, the material, the *physique* of our
pleasures, by veiling these ideas, by forgetting them
altogether, or, at least, never naming them hardly
to one's self, that we alone can prevent them from
disgusting.

(Journal entry, 13 December 1813)

That's what Juan was doing when he thought of the
'boundless skies' alongside 'Julia's eyes', and it's what
we all do some of the time, for everyone is awkwardly
stationed between being a mind that acts on a body,
and a body that seems to have a mind of its own. Byron
may say that we veil, or forget, or never quite name our
compromised natures to ourselves, but passages like
this actually help us to keep such things in mind and to
manage our conflicts by acknowledging them. Reading
Byron is an exercise in becoming a 'true voluptuary',

which means becoming open to having mixed feelings about feelings.

There are other reasons to be attentive to bodies. 'I can recognize any one by the teeth, with whom I have talked,' Byron said. 'I always watch the lips and mouth: they tell what the tongue and eyes try to conceal.' And, as might be expected, a poet with a club foot is very sensitive to feet. He notes of the princess Gulbeyaz that 'there was a self-will even in her small feet':

> She stopt, and raised her head to speak – but paused,
> And then moved on again with rapid pace;
> Then slackened it, which is the march most caused
> By deep Emotion: – you may sometimes trace
> A feeling in each footstep
>
> (*Don Juan*, 1819–24)

The lines suggest not only that Gulbeyaz's emotions cause her changes in pace, but also that she is somehow doing her thinking and feeling with her feet. It's as though she is now taking soundings from her bodily rhythms to work out what her ideas are, or even as though her feet might have or give her ideas. The aside is noteworthy too: '*you* may sometimes trace'. By 'you' Byron usually means 'everyone', and here readers are asked to take time to listen to their bodies in order to trace – and perhaps even to change – their minds. A mindful awareness of the body can combat recur-

rent depression or anger, and we can use our bodies
– modulating our breath, for example – to alter our
mood. Gulbeyaz was about 'to speak – but paused'.
That pause is for thought – the body's thought.

Sensitivity to body matters needn't always be a curse.
Simply trying to imagine what it might be like for the
person next to you to inhabit their own body can lead
to an extension of your sympathies, and Byron himself
had an insatiable appetite for other people's experiences. ('I should like to know', he said, 'how a person
feels after committing a murder.') His foot prevented
him from dancing, but it didn't prevent him from
delighting in dance – and from pondering the ways in
which dance provides us with a model of how to form
connections. Sometimes dance is foreplay:

> Through the full veins thy gentler poison swims,
> And wakes to wantonness the willing limbs . . .
> Round all the confines of the yielded waist,
> The strangest hand may wander undisplaced . . .
> And true, though strange – Waltz whispers this
>   remark,
> 'My slippery steps are safest in the dark!'
> (The Waltz, 1813)

On other occasions, dance gestures towards a different
kind of consummation. Here is Don Juan taking to
the floor:

And then he danced; – all foreigners excel
    The serious Angles in the eloquence
Of pantomime; – he danced, I say, right well,
    With emphasis, and also with good sense –
A thing in footing indispensable:
    He danced without theatrical pretence,
Not like a ballet-master in the van
Of his drilled nymphs, but like a gentleman.

                                    (*Don Juan*, 1819–24)

Dance, we could say, is a form of thinking with your body, and good dancing involves cooperation, give and take. For Byron, the tactility of dance is also a form of tact: 'I consider tact the real *panacea* of life,' he said. 'Our tact is always in proportion to our sensibility.' So physiology may be linked to ethics if we see our bodies as part of the body politic. Juan's 'footing' refers not only to the physical placement of feet, but also to a form of social cooperation – as when we put ourselves on the same footing with others.

Juan dances with 'good sense' (recall Byron's feeling that the poet should appeal 'To the good sense and senses of mankind') – which would make reading a kind of dance, as the writer and philosopher Maurice Blanchot once suggested: 'Reading is perhaps in fact a dance with an invisible partner in a separated space.' What we can take from a turn with Byron is the idea that we put our best foot forward when we try not to be too knowing about what our or other people's bodies should want, be, and do – or about what they are capable of. The poet once confessed that 'an addiction to poetry is very generally the result of "an uneasy mind in an uneasy body"', but one way to deal with the unease is to imagine what new purposes you could make it serve. The physiognomy of words is similarly malleable when subject to poetic play: an anagram of 'uneasy' is 'any use'.

To think with your body is to keep the mind active by keeping it moving. Wittgenstein once noted: 'I find it important in philosophizing to keep changing my posture, not to stand for too long on one leg, so as not to get stiff.' When mulling over his own posture in relation to somebody he wasn't particularly fond of, Byron found philosophic words that are worth bearing in mind whenever we're reflecting on the thorns in our own sides (awkward relatives, say, or bankers – or a combination of both horrors). As so often with Byron, an inclination towards judgement is answered by a vision of embodied process: 'Opinions are made to be changed – or how is truth to be got at? we don't arrive at it by standing on one leg.'

3

HOW TO LAUGH

....

> You know, laughing is the sign of a rational animal,
> so says Dr. Smollett. I think so too, but unluckily my
> spirits don't always keep pace with my opinions.
> (Byron, letter to Francis Hodgson,
> 3 November 1808)

Laughing may be the sign of a rational animal, but laughter is itself an ungovernable, unruly creature. It often arrives when it shouldn't (when, for example, we disingenuously protest: 'It wasn't me!') and laughs can't always be summoned when they're needed (our friends' bad jokes). Byron's comments to his friend Hodgson were part of an account about the moment he found himself seated at dinner next to an old flame, Mary Chaworth (now Mrs Chaworth-Musters):

> I had not so much scope for risibility the other day
> as I could have wished . . . I was determined to be
> valiant, and converse with "sang froid," but instead I
> forgot my valour and nonchalance, and never opened
> my lips even to laugh, far less to speak, & the Lady

was almost as absurd as myself, which made both the object of more observation, than if we had conducted ourselves with easy indifference. – You will think all this great nonsense, if you had seen it you would have thought it still more ridiculous. – What fools we!

(Letter to Francis Hodgson, 3 November 1808)

Byron once referred to 'the *comedy* of the passions'. Our passions – especially the unrequited kind – often feel more like a tragicomedy, but the poet's phrasing hints at the possibility that intense feeling could be better enjoyed (or endured) if it could be seen as somehow laughable. It's noteworthy that the passage above begins on 'I' and ends on 'we', moving from a personal confession to a broader insight: 'What fools we!' includes both the couple at dinner and people in general. The lesson learned here might be rephrased as a question and response: in T. S. Eliot's *The Cocktail Party*, an exasperated Edward says to the doctor, 'Don't you see that it makes me ridiculous?' and the doctor replies:

It will do you no harm to find yourself ridiculous.
Resign yourself to be the fool you are.

(T. S. Eliot, The Cocktail Party, 1949)

Byron gravitates towards this kind of wisdom, and towards other questions which it raises: Are there good and bad ways to cherish the ridiculous? If some types of laugh are offered as cures, will they cure us of other things we might value or need? How should we take – and provoke – laughter?

No use denying it: Byron frequently reminds us how much fun it is to laugh – at others. When asked to describe his doctor, the poet said: 'He was exactly the kind of person to whom, if he fell overboard, one would hold out a straw to know if the adage be true that drowning men catch at straws.' Elsewhere, he reported: 'The Cardinal is at his wit's end – it is true that he had not far to go.' Our own wit can be a weapon; we laugh at others to teach them the error of their ways, or simply to delight in the fact that they – and not we – have made the error (spilled drinks, Freudian slips, unseen banana skins). But Byron also ponders what else lies behind our relish for ridicule. His wife noted that 'the greater the levity of Lord Byron's compositions, the more I imagine him to suffer from the turbid state of his mind', and the poet himself confessed that 'some of my nearest approaches to the comic have been written under a deep depression of spirits'. So we might see the comic perspective as an evasion or displacement of something. As Byron later wrote:

if I laugh at any mortal thing,
'Tis that I may not weep.

(*Don Juan*, 1819–24)

Certainly, when the heroes of Byron's early poems laugh, they do so in weird ways:

> Yet oft-times in his maddest mirthful mood
> Strange pangs would flash along Childe Harold's
> brow.
>
> *(Childe Harold's Pilgrimage*, 1812–18)

Conrad is even odder:

> There was a laughing devil in his sneer . . .
> Strange though it seem – yet with extremest grief
> Is linked a mirth – it doth not bring relief –
> That playfulness of Sorrow ne'er beguiles,
> And smiles in bitterness – but still it smiles;
> And sometimes with the wisest and the best,
> Till even the scaffold echoes with their jest! . . .
> Whate'er it was that flashed on Conrad, now
> A laughing wildness half unbent his brow:
> And these his accents had a sound of mirth,
> As if the last he could enjoy on earth
>
> *(The Corsair*, 1814)

This eerie mirth is offered as an emblem of a more general insight: some laughs feel like last resorts. Perhaps, then, we laugh at others in order to shift our own worry or unease onto them. The nervous smile or bitter laugh may be an avoidance of our own emotional engagements, a way to reduce or to repress the feeling that we are somehow implicated in a situation. But Byron suggests that this coping mechanism 'doth not bring relief'. 'I strove / To laugh the thought away, but 'twould not be', says Lioni in *Marino Faliero* (1821). And in *Lara*, the hero's recourse to sarcasm doesn't get rid of whatever's bothering him:

> The smile might reach his lip, but passed not by,
> None e'er could trace its laughter to his eye.
>
> (*Lara*, 1814)

Byron encourages us to wonder what might happen if we were to stop using laughter as a kind of displaced violence – as something we do to other people when we feel vulnerable – and tried to see ourselves as a *part* of what's laughable. After all, nobody ever truly has the last laugh, as *Don Juan* reminds us:

> Death laughs – Go ponder o'er the skeleton
>   With which men image out the unknown thing
> That hides the past world, like to a set sun
>   Which still elsewhere may rouse a brighter
>   spring, –
> Death laughs at all you weep for:– look upon
>   This hourly dread of all, whose *threatened sting*

Turns life to terror, even though in its sheath!
Mark! how its lipless mouth grins without breath!

Mark how it laughs and scorns at all you are!
    And yet *was* what you are: from *ear* to *ear*
It *laughs not* – there is now no fleshy bar
    So called; the Antic long hath ceased to *hear*,
But still he *smiles*; and whether near or far,
    He strips from man that mantle (far more dear
Than even the tailor's), his incarnate skin,
White, black, or copper – the dead bones will grin.

And thus Death laughs, – it is sad merriment,
    But still it *is* so; and with such example
Why should not Life be equally content,
    With his Superior, in a smile to trample
Upon the nothings which are daily spent
    Like bubbles on an ocean much less ample
Than the eternal deluge, which devours
Suns as rays – worlds like atoms – years like hours?

                              (*Don Juan*, 1819–24)

The shift here from what 'men' imagine to what 'you' weep for underlines the fact that this skeleton is really the one in *our* closet. Laughter is a memento mori: we're all in the same boat, and it appears to be sinking. That said, it transpires that Life might be Death's equal if we could sometimes conjure up a sense of humour that sees all concerns – our own included – as equally insignificant.

> They accuse me – *Me* – the present writer of
>> The present poem – of – I know not what, –
> A tendency to under-rate and scoff
>> At human power and virtue, and all that . . .
>
> When we know what we all are, we must bewail us,
>> But ne'ertheless, I hope it is no crime
> To laugh at *all* things – for I wish to know
> *What* after *all*, are *all* things – but a *Show*?
>> (*Don Juan*, 1819–24)

This particular Byronic laugh might be a gift, not a curse. To be told that you overrate your own 'power and virtue, and all that' seems initially like a put-down, but it can free you from having to worry so much. Self-importance takes effort. Laughter can be a way of taking time off from the fretful, wearying business of maintaining a respectable self-image.

'*What* after *all*, are *all* things – but a *Show*?' This may suggest that everything is a deception, but a show is also a play, or performance, or entertainment. And the show must go on. 'There is no comedy after all like real life,' Byron wrote, so to live your life as a comedy is to get real:

39

Now at length we're off for Turkey,
    Lord knows when we shall come back.
Breezes foul, and tempest murky,
    May unship us in a crack.
But since life at most a jest is,
    As Philosophers allow,
Still to laugh by far the best is,
    Then laugh on – as I do now.
    Laugh at all things,
    Great and small things,
Sick or well, at sea or shore,
    While we're quaffing
    Let's have laughing,
Who the Devil cares for more?

('Lines to Mr. Hodgson', 1809)

This devil-may-care attitude *does* care for laughter. It's as though laughter were a reliable friend or an ally who has our best interests at heart. In this imagining, our laughter raises the spirits by refusing to let us become too knowing about whatever we think it is that life owes us (a living; happiness; our place in the queue). Byron later confessed:

I am afraid that this sounds flippant, but I don't mean it to be so; only my turn of mind is so given to taking things in the absurd point of

view, that it breaks out in spite of me every now
and then.

(Letter to Thomas Moore, 8 March 1822)

Every now and then, that absurd point of view breaks
out so that we can take a break from ourselves.

Alexander Pope noted that 'there is a difference
betwixt laughing *about* a thing and laughing *at* a thing',
and Byron's hope is that if people can learn to laugh
about their own limitations, they may become less
inclined to use laughter to separate themselves from
others. In an early satirical work, the poet paused
briefly from poking fun at enemies to imagine what his
audience might make of him:

some kind, censorious friend will say,
'What, art thou better, meddling fool, than they?'
(*English Bards and Scotch Reviewers*, 1809)

Revising the poem many years later, Byron added a foot-
note: '*Fool* enough, certainly, then, and no wiser since.'
So resigning himself to be the fool he is has changed his
attitude to the follies of those around him. In *Don Juan*
he acknowledges that 'even my Muse's worst reproof's
a smile', and elsewhere he envisages laughter not as
a signal that the moral high ground has been gained,
but as a confession that the subject and the object

of laughter are on intimate terms: 'Do not suppose because I laughed then – that I had no feeling for him or for myself.' Many of Byron's best jokes arrive when he casts ironic side-glances at his own reflection in the mirror whilst at the same time pondering his relationships with others: he writes of a new lover that 'her great merit is finding out mine – there is nothing so amiable as discernment'. Later, on the eve of his wedding, he reports: 'I am about to be married – and am of course in all the misery of a man in pursuit of happiness.'

One of Byron's admirers, the poet Fernando Pessoa, defined humour as 'the consciousness that what is laughable is akin to ourselves'. This is the kind of humour that Byron tries to coax out of us, and it brings with it a laughter that renounces the pleasures of satirical point-scoring in favour of another kind of activity:

> I fear I have a little turn for satire,
>   And yet methinks the older that one grows
> Inclines us more to laugh than scold, though laughter
> Leaves us so doubly serious shortly after.
>
> (*Beppo*, 1818)

The movement of this passage echoes that of the letter to Hodgson with which this chapter began. The lines begin with a personal 'I', then journey to the more general 'one', before finally arriving at an inclusive sense of 'us'. It's Byron's way of sharing a perspective and a joke, his way of saying that laughter is something to be done *with* and not *to* people. Some forms of laughter intimate that we are less distant from each other than we might think. We can be doubled up or doubled over by laughter, but a good laugh leaves us 'doubly serious' because it reminds us of just how much we yearn to be part of a double act.

4

HOW TO
GO ASTRAY

....

MYRRHA: I would remain: I have no happiness
Save in beholding thine; yet –

SARDANAPALUS: Yet! what YET?

(Byron, *Sardanapalus*, 1821)

There are plenty of lessons in how *not* to go astray. Many self-help mantras – how to *go one better* in business, for example, or how to *go further* in personal relationships – envisage the march of time as synonymous with progress. The new is the improved; older is wiser; people don't just grow, but grow *up*. To be *going places* is to be directed, purposeful, assured. And if you're described as having *get up and go*, it's generally assumed that you know where you're going *to*.

Wherever we turn, we are pleased (and plagued) by authorities who claim that our lives should have developmental plot lines, and Byron too acknowledges 'the sad consequence of going astray'. In his 'Epistle to Augusta', he bemoans the fact that, from birth, he had 'a fate, or will, that walked astray', and much of his writing mulls over the sad consequence of going – or being led – off the straight and narrow:

> "Kiss" rhymes to "bliss" in fact as well as verse –
> I wish it never led to something worse.
>
> (*Don Juan*, 1819–24)

In *Beppo*, he explains what that something might be:

> For glances beget ogles, ogles sighs,
>   Sighs wishes, wishes words, and words a letter,
> Which flies on wing of light-heeled Mercuries,
>   Who do such things because they know no better;
> And then, God knows, what mischief may arise,
>   When love links two young people in one fetter,
> Vile assignations, and adulterous beds,
> Elopements, broken vows, and hearts, and heads.
>
> (*Beppo*, 1818)

Sounds messy. Yet Byron's poetry often revels in our *need* to lose our heads. In *Don Juan*, readers are invited to eavesdrop on Julia and Juan, a couple who have resolved to keep their hands to themselves (Julia is a married woman):

> And Julia sate with Juan, half embraced
>   And half retiring from the glowing arm,

Which trembled like the bosom where 'twas placed;
    Yet still she must have thought there was no harm,
Or else 'twere easy to withdraw her waist;
    But then the situation had its charm,
And then -- God knows what next -- I can't go on;
I'm almost sorry that I e'er begun . . .

And Julia's voice was lost, except in sighs,
    Until too late for useful conversation;
The tears were gushing from her gentle eyes,
    I wish, indeed, they had not had occasion,
But who, alas! can love, and then be wise?
    Not that remorse did not oppose temptation,
A little still she strove, and much repented,
And whispering 'I will ne'er consent' – consented.

(Don Juan, 1819–24)

The poet and Julia are partners in crime here. He says: 'I can't go on' with the story, and she says: 'I will ne'er consent,' but both parties want to complete the thing they've started (he the stanza, she the kiss). And we too are keen for the rhymes – and the people – to come together. The whole thing feels so wrong it's right, which prompts some questions: Can going astray be good for us? Might we have cause to repent our lack of temptations? Is there a way of conceiving the good life as one that isn't entirely in tune with its own principles – or not wholly sure of where it's going?

Later on in the 'Epistle to Augusta', the poet says to his sister that he wishes for 'a world to roam through, and a home with you'. The home / roam rhyme marks a dual allegiance, but the more you read Byron, the more you get the feeling that 'roam' – not 'home' – is where the heart is. For this poet, lack of motion is hardly ever a good sign:

> The rivers, lakes, and ocean all stood still . . .
> The waves were dead; the tides were in their grave.
>
> ('Darkness', 1816)

Byron's heroes have a 'slakeless thirst of change', and they speak for whatever it is in us that needs to challenge or to avoid comfort, rather than to find it:

> To horse! to horse! he quits, for ever quits
> A scene of peace, though soothing to his soul:
> Again he rouses from his moping fits,
> But seeks not now the harlot and the bowl.
> Onward he flies, nor fixed as yet the goal
> Where he shall rest him on his pilgrimage;
> And o'er him many changing scenes must roll
> Ere toil his thirst for travel can assuage,
> Or he shall calm his breast, or learn experience sage.
>
> (*Childe Harold's Pilgrimage*, 1812–18)

Byron often suggests that the most valuable pilgrimages (and lives) don't really have goals. Passion is 'the poetry of life', he wrote, and to live life *as* poetry is to live it as something both invigorating and unsettling: 'A man must travel, and turmoil, or there is no existence.' We often travel to get away from it all, or simply to get to where we want to go. But Byron asks readers to entertain a form of transport that is neither fleeing from, nor looking forward to, anything. Instead, he recommends an intense form of going astray. Errancy is energy:

> Now there is nothing gives a man such spirits,
>   Leavening his blood as Cayenne doth a curry,
> As going at full speed – no matter where its
>   Direction be, so 'tis but in a hurry,
> And merely for the sake of its own merits:
>   For the less cause there is for all this flurry,
> The greater is the pleasure in arriving
> At the great *end* of travel – which is driving.
>   (*Don Juan*, 1819–24)

The less defined the cause, the greater the pleasure. It's as though we might inhabit our lives more fully by refusing to think of the future as a home, or destination, or conclusion at which we need to arrive.

Don Juan is over 127,000 words long, but not once does it have recourse to the words 'develop', or 'development', or 'developing'. Digression is more Byron's style, and the style asks us to embrace – rather than merely to endure – a life that isn't plotted:

> Accept, then, my concession
> In truth, dear Clare, in fancy's flight
> I soar along from left to right,
> My Muse admires digression.
>
> ('To the Earl of Clare', 1807)

Our eyes soar along from left to right too, so this makes it sound as though reading might itself be a kind of digression or going astray. In the first canto of *Don Juan*, it appears that we are on the straight and narrow – at least, it seems so before we reach the last line of this stanza:

> My way is to begin with the beginning;
> The regularity of my design
> Forbids all wandering as the worst of sinning,
> And therefore I shall open with a line
> (Although it cost me half an hour in spinning)
> Narrating somewhat of Don Juan's father,
> And also of his mother, if you'd rather.
>
> (*Don Juan*, 1819–24)

For Byron, wandering is wondering – and, in particular, wondering about what our need for stories, plots and 'meanings' might be keeping us from:

> But to my tale of Laura, – for I find
>   Digression is a sin, that by degrees
> Becomes exceeding tedious to my mind,
>   And, therefore, may the reader too displease –
> The gentle reader, who may wax unkind,
>   And caring little for the author's ease,
> Insist on knowing what he means, a hard
> And hapless situation for a bard.
>
> *(Beppo*, 1818)

He writes this whilst smiling at us because he knows that we *want* him to digress – partly because we want, from time to time, to be allowed to digress ourselves. A digression is a 'diversion' in the full sense of that word; it diverts and pleases by allowing us time off from the tiresome business of trying to know what other people – and ourselves – are meant to 'mean'.

Byron wrote to a friend: 'You must not mind occasional rambling – I mean *Don Juan* for a poetical *Tristram Shandy* – or Montaigne's Essays with a story for hinge.' In *Tristram Shandy*, the narrator observes: 'Digressions, incontestably, are the sunshine; – they are the life, the soul of reading!' The Renaissance essayist Montaigne informs one addressee that 'I have so far digressed, the better to divert you', and elsewhere he adds:

> Gently bending my discourse, and by little and little digressing, sometimes to subjects nearer,

> and sometimes more remote from the purpose,
> according as she was more intent on what I said, I
> imperceptibly led her from that sorrowful thought,
> and kept her calm and in good humour whilst I
> continued there. I herein made use of diversion . . .
> We always think of something else . . . Variation ever
> relieves, dissolves, and dissipates . . . If I am not able
> to contend with it, I escape from it . . . I secure myself
> in the crowd of other thoughts and fancies.
>
> (Montaigne, 'Of Diversion', 1580)

This is very close to the Byronic way of being in the world. *Don Juan* often changes the subject as a way of coaxing us out of our fixations. Both the characters and the narrator often seem to have lost the plot, but the poem suggests that there may be worse things to lose than this – your sense of humour, say, or your sense of perspective.

Nearly every time Byron goes astray with a digression, he apologizes, before then suggesting that he's not really apologizing:

> Kind reader! pass
> This long parenthesis: I could not shut
> It sooner for the soul of me, and class
> My faults even with your own! which meaneth, Put
> A kind construction upon them and me:
> But *that* you won't – then don't – I am not less free.

. . .

Oh pardon my digression – or at least
　　Peruse! 'Tis always with a moral end
That I dissert
　　　　　　　　　　　(*Don Juan*, 1819–24)

The moral end of digression is a lesson about our love-affair with endings and with progress narratives, with how we use our life stories to limit what our lives actually are – or might be. Going astray, digressing or being distracted needn't be seen as failings; they can be ways to foster creativity. As Roland Barthes put it: 'To be with the one I love and to think of something else – this is how I have my best ideas.'

By staging and then sabotaging the need for a polished story, Byron encourages readers to take pleasure at not being equal to our 'life plan' (whatever that is). Being at a loss is seen as a kind of gain. 'Where do you see yourself in five years' time?' interviewers often ask. Byron isn't sure where he sees himself in the next five lines:

I ne'er decide what I shall say, and this I call
　　Much too poetical. Men should know why
They write, and for what end; but, note or text,
I never know the word which will come next.
　　　　　　　　　　　(*Don Juan*, 1819–24)

We don't really believe that he believes that 'Men should know why / They write, and for what end'. Or rather, we don't believe that he feels this all the time. (His close friend Thomas Medwin reported of the poet: 'He told me that, when he wrote, he neither knew nor cared what was coming next.') Not the least of Byron's virtues is that he makes knowingness seem boring. To his infuriated publisher he wrote: 'You ask me for the plan of Donny Johnny – I *have* no plan – I *had* no plan – but I had or have materials.' The poet suggests that it's a relief not to have a plan, and also that it's a kind of plucky resistance:

> My Muses do not care a pinch of rosin
>   About what's called success, or not succeeding:
> Such thoughts are quite below the strain they have
>   chosen;
>   'Tis a 'great moral lesson' they are reading.
> I thought, at setting off, about two dozen
>   Cantos would do; but at Apollo's pleading,
> If that my Pegasus should not be foundered,
> I think to canter gently through a hundred . . .
>
> Here the twelfth Canto of our introduction
>   Ends. When the body of the book's begun,
> You'll find it of a different construction
>   From what some people say 'twill be when done:
> The plan at present's simply in concoction.

> I can't oblige you, reader! to read on;
> That's your affair, not mine: a real spirit
> Should neither court neglect nor dread to bear it.
>
> (*Don Juan*, 1819–24)

If, as John Lennon claimed, 'life is what happens to you while you're busy making other plans', then one way to grab hold of a little more life is to keep plans provisional – or 'in concoction'. A 'real spirit' is somebody who refuses to let others dictate his story (or his life story) to him. The great moral lesson we are reading is a lesson in how to resist the lure of the success story. The poet's phrasing is significant: he doesn't care for '*what's called* success, or not succeeding' – partly because what's so often called success is so oppressive. Chekhov was in agreement with Byron on this score; regarding the notion that you could divide people up into 'successful' and 'unsuccessful' types, he once wrote to a friend: 'Are you successful or aren't you? What about me? What about Napoleon? One would need to be a god to distinguish successful from unsuccessful people without making mistakes. I'm going to a dance.'

Byron often reminds us that our lives are indebted to other lives going astray. Take, for example, the Russian general Koutousow, who became renowned for defeating Napoleon's Grande Armée in 1812. In *Don Juan*, we join him at the siege of Ismail in 1790. Byron reports:

> Koutousow, he who afterward beat back
> 　(With some assistance from the frost and snow)
> Napoleon on his bold and bloody track,
> 　It happened was himself beat back just now.
> 　　　　　　　　　　　　(*Don Juan*, 1819–24)

Just as it looks as though he will suffer an ignominious death in a ditch, along with his column of men, he gets lucky:

> And had it not been for some stray troops, landing
> 　They knew not where, being carried by the stream
> To some spot, where they lost their understanding,
> 　And wandered up and down as in a dream,
> Until they reached, as day-break was expanding,
> 　That which a portal to their eyes did seem, —
> The great and gay Koutousow might have lain
> Where three parts of his column yet remain.
> 　　　　　　　　　　　　(*Don Juan*, 1819–24)

Losing our understanding, straying from what we know, can be a blessing in disguise – a reminder of just how much of life is based on serendipity, chance, contingency. We wander 'up and down as in a dream', and we dream – as we may learn to live – less knowingly, with our unconscious leading us astray to unforeseen outcomes. This is also what Byron felt his own writing encouraged: 'As for poesy, mine is the *dream* of my sleeping Passions – when they are awake, I cannot speak their language.' Dreams allow us to speak a different language, to be surprised by our passions, and many of our most cherished moments are surprises. Or detours. Or gifts. Or luck. Or side effects. To go astray is to allow more of these moments into our lives.

5

HOW TO
GET WET

....

There are lots of ways we'd rather *not* get wet: standing next to a puddle as the bus we were running for passes us by; stepping into a cold shower; living in England. (In *Beppo*, Byron noted of his native land: 'I like the weather, when it is not rainy, / That is, I like two months of every year.') Still, the poet did like getting into deep water. He was a superb swimmer, once treading water for four hours without touching land. He also swam the Hellespont – as he reminds us when talking about Juan:

A better swimmer you could scarce see ever,
    He could, perhaps, have pass'd the Hellespont,
As once (a feat on which ourselves we prided)
Leander, Mr. Ekenhead, and I did.

(*Don Juan*, 1819–24)

Byron's other heroes are often looking seawards:

> Once more upon the waters! yet once more!
> And the waves bound beneath me as a steed
> That knows his rider. Welcome, to their roar!
> Swift be their guidance, wheresoe'er it lead!
> (*Childe Harold's Pilgrimage*, 1812–18)

There's an intriguing mixture of mastery and passivity here. The rider would seem to control the steed, but when the waves start to roar they become untameable, taking control of the rider and leading him where they will. Might such a grand welcome to the watery offer a lesson about the value of a fluid approach to life? Certainly, whenever Harold imagines being *on* the sea, or taking charge of it, his thoughts soon turn to imagining himself *in* it, and submitting to it:

> Roll on, thou deep and dark blue ocean – roll!
> Ten thousand fleets sweep over thee in vain;
> Man marks the earth with ruin – his control
> Stops with the shore . . .
>
> And I have loved thee, Ocean! and my joy
> Of youthful sports was on thy breast to be
> Borne, like thy bubbles, onward: from a boy
> I wantoned with thy breakers – they to me
> Were a delight; and if the freshening sea

Made them a terror – 'twas a pleasing fear,

For I was as it were a child of thee,

And trusted to thy billows far and near,

And laid my hand upon thy mane – as I do here.

(*Childe Harold's Pilgrimage*, 1812–18)

First 'delight', then 'terror', then 'pleasing fear'. Swimming isn't just a mark of physical prowess, but a way of risking something, relinquishing control, letting go. The last line implies that the poet sees the act of writing (and perhaps of living) as analogous with swimming. So what aspect of ourselves does water put us in touch with? Can getting wet be read as a metaphor for getting something more out of life? Philosopher Gaston Bachelard suggests that a person dedicated to water is a person in flux, and that uncertain waters offer what he calls 'a schema for courage':

A leap into the unknown is a leap into water . . . One dives into water in order to be reborn and changed . . . Hydrotherapeutics is not simply peripheral . . . The contemplation and experience of water lead us, by many routes, to an ideal. We should not underestimate the lessons taught by original matters. They have left their mark on our mind's youth.

(*Water and Dreams: An Essay on the Imagination of Matter*, translated by Edith R. Farrell, 1983)

What are these lessons? And how does our poet imagine the ethics of hydrotherapeutics? When we dive into the book of Byron, what are we diving into?

One answer might be: our earlier selves. Writer and film-maker Roger Deakin has observed that 'I know of few people and no poet for whom water is not a first love'. In Byron's work, the recollection of water often reacquaints people with their youth, and replenishes them with it:

> How many a time have I
> Cloven with arm still lustier, breast more daring,
> The wave all roughened; with a swimmer's stroke
> Flinging the billows back from my drenched hair,
> And laughing from my lip the audacious brine,
> Which kissed it like a wine-cup, rising oe'r
> The waves as they arose, and prouder still
> The loftier they uplifted me . . .
>
> > – I was a boy then.
> > (*The Two Foscari*, 1821)

To get wet in this way is to fill your cup, to get drunk on the sea. The pleasure feels intoxicating. (Byron wrote *Don Juan* having wet his whistle. 'It was all *gin*,' he said. 'Gin-and-water is the source of all my inspiration . . . the true Hippocrene.') It's also erotic (all lusty arms and daring breasts), and that 'stroke' is suggestive too.

Yet it's only a swim, and what could be more innocent than going for a swim? Byron frequently encourages us to view our sensuality as *shameless*, in the best sense of that word:

> Juan was quite 'a broth of a boy,'
>   A thing of impulse and a child of song;
> Now swimming in the sentiment of joy,
>   Or the sensation (if that phrase seem wrong)
>   (*Don Juan*, 1819–24)

A 'broth' of a boy: a distinctly deliquescent youth, then. For Byron, the sentimental is often too *mental*, not elemental enough. So he invites his characters – and readers – to swim in sensations, to surrender to experience. His stanzas describing Juan and Haidee's relationship are full of lovely liquidities:

> And slowly by his swimming eyes was seen
> A lovely female face of seventeen . . .
>
> He was her own, her ocean-treasure, cast
> Like a rich wreck – her first love, and her last . . .
>
> Juan, after bathing in the sea,
> Came always back to coffee and Haidee . . .
>   (*Don Juan*, 1819–24)

Which is to say, he drinks in both coffee *and* Haidee, just as she swallowed him up with her eyes when she first saw him washed up by the ocean. Byron is always enthusiastic about the slippery. He admires the Italian language for its 'gentle liquids', and the Italian women for their 'wild and liquid glance':

> oh! the loveliness at times we see
>   In momentary gliding.
>
> *(Beppo*, 1818)

Water recalls us to whatever is wild in us, reminds us what we are made of. One of Byron's heroes loves to listen to the ocean for this reason:

>   his wild spirit wilder wishes sent
> Roused by the roar of his own element!
>
> *(The Corsair*, 1814)

So we should get wet to be roused, aroused, ruffled. Some early reviewers of *Don Juan* complained that the poem wasn't true to experience because it blended different states and moods, linked pleasure and pain, levity and seriousness, and made life generally seem more confusing than it really needed to be. One critic put the point by saying that, in real life, 'we are never scorched and drenched at the same time'. The poet begged to differ:

> Blessings on his experience! . . . Did he never walk a
> mile in hot weather? Did he never spill a dish of tea
> over his testicles in handing a cup to his charmer,
> to the great shame of his nankeen breeches? Did he
> never swim in the sea at Noonday with the Sun in
> his eyes and on his head, which all the foam of the
> Ocean could not cool?
>
> (Letter to John Murray, 12 August 1819)

Byron encourages us to have experiences that we can't
quite make up our minds about. The ocean is a vital
image for him in this respect because it seems so vari-
able, so beyond imagining. We go to the ocean to escape
(a day out at the seaside, perhaps), but the poet also
suggests that we go there to experience more fully *that
which escapes us*. In a note to *Childe Harold's Pilgrimage*,
he wrote that 'a painting can give no sufficient idea of
the ocean', and he would later speak of 'life's ocean' –
which may imply that we are only really living our life
when we feel all at sea (in *Don Juan* he refers to 'our
nautical existence'). The poet Swinburne's response
to *Don Juan* is worth quoting at length here because
it suggests that the poem's very style is offering us a
vision of the good life – or, as Bachelard put it, that
'the contemplation and experience of water lead us, by
many routes, to an ideal':

This perpetual change, this tidal variety of experience and emotion, gives to the poem something of the breadth and freshness of the sea ... Across the stanzas of *Don Juan* we swim forward as over 'the broad backs of the sea'; they break and glitter, hiss and laugh, murmur and move, like waves that sound and subside. There is in them a delicious resistance, an elastic motion, which salt water has and fresh water has not. There is about them a wide wholesome air, full of vivid light and constant wind, which is only felt at sea ... Here, as at sea, there is enough and too much of fluctuation and intermission; the ripple flags and falls in loose and lazy lines; the foam flies wide of any mark, and breakers collapse here and there in sudden ruin and violent failure. But the violence and the weakness of the sea are preferable to the smooth sound and equable security of a lake ... There are others whom it sickens, and others whom it chills; these will do well to steer inshore.

(Preface to *Selection from the Works of Lord Byron*, 1866)

This is profoundly in tune with how Byron hears the call of the sea in our lives. The call could be metaphorical or real (ideally, both), but in whichever form it comes, it asks to be heeded. 'Anything', he said, 'but a dull cruise on a level lake without ever losing sight

of the same insipid shores by which it is surrounded.'
To the Lake Poets who (Byron claimed) felt they had a
monopoly on poetic excellence, he responded:

> There is a narrowness in such a notion
> Which makes me wish you'd change your lakes for
> ocean.
>
> (Dedication to *Don Juan*, 1819–24)

So the ocean makes us a little more liberal by exposing
us to what Swinburne terms 'enough and too much of
fluctuation and intermission'. To get wet is to get out
more, to submit to another element, and to do this
can be to gain an appetite for liberty. One of Byron's
favourite rhymes is 'free / sea'. In *Mazeppa*, he cele-
brates 'the wild, the free, / Like waves that follow o'er
the sea', and *The Corsair* begins:

> O'er the glad waters of the dark blue sea,
> Our thoughts as boundless, and our souls as free . . .
> Ours the wild life in tumult still to range
> From toil to rest, and joy in every change . . .
> Oh, who can tell, save he whose heart hath tried,
> And danced in triumph o'er the waters wide,
> The exulting sense – the pulse's maddening play,
> That thrills the wanderer of that trackless way?
>
> (*The Corsair*, 1814)

These lines communicate something that is often present in Byron: the feeling that committing ourselves to an environment or setting allows us to partake of its energy (to have 'thoughts as boundless . . . souls as free' as the ocean itself). The pulse's maddening play is a miniature version of the waves around us. Coleridge was getting at a similar feeling when he wrote to a friend: 'My whole Being is filled with waves, as it were, that roll & stumble, one this way, & one that way, like things that have no common master.' For Byron, I think, imagining yourself in this way can make you less likely to want to master others; it's as though by submerging yourself in your own unfathomable, fluid nature, you can learn to become more tolerant of others (or less tolerant of intolerance). The aqueous self is a more equable one.

When the poet turns to politics, the ocean becomes the image of a liberty we should all help to make:

It is not one man, nor a million, but the *spirit* of liberty which must be spread. The waves which dash upon the shore are, one by one, broken, but yet the *ocean* conquers, nevertheless. It overwhelms the Armada, it wears the rock . . . In like manner, whatever the sacrifice of individuals, the great cause will gather strength, sweep down what is rugged, and fertilize (for *sea-weed* is *manure*) what is cultivable.

(Ravenna Journal, 9 January 1821)

So the sexual turns social here. The earlier energies of those 'gentle liquids' (seminal, perhaps; lubricants, certainly) now give rise to other versions of fertility. To get wet is to join in.

The lesson of water is finally a lesson about how to learn to live with – and to enjoy – a mixed feeling of our limited power alongside our unlimited potential. This is close to the feeling we began with in *Childe Harold's Pilgrimage*, where the sea-bound hero was both rider and ridden. In *Don Juan*, one canto ends like this:

> Between two worlds life hovers like a star,
>   'Twixt night and morn, upon the horizon's verge:
> How little do we know that which we are!
>   How less what we may be! The eternal surge
> Of time and tide rolls on, and bears afar
>   Our bubbles; as the old burst, new emerge,
> Lashed from the foam of ages; while the graves
> Of Empires heave but like some passing waves.
>
> (*Don Juan*, 1819–24)

From this perspective, the tides make all our tidings seem insignificant. Byron frequently returns to the image of his own writing as related to water, and to a sense of how little our words may matter in the grand scheme of things. The last stanza of the first canto sends off his book with a blessing, 'I cast thee on the waters – go thy ways,' and later he adds:

And what I write I cast upon the stream,
To swim or sink – I have had at least my dream.

(*Don Juan*, 1819–24)

It's as though the poem is imagined as a fragile message in a bottle, and we may get a sinking feeling here about the powers of even the most eloquent forms of expression. And yet Byron's viscous imagination mixes this image in solution with another:

But words are things, and a small drop of ink,
    Falling like dew, upon a thought, produces
That which makes thousands, perhaps millions,
    think.

(*Don Juan*, 1819–24)

The poet's writing is an emblem of effort amid tricky conditions, and a vision of how even a small gesture can have unforeseen, incalculably diffusive effects. Perhaps the best way to get wet is to accept that, while we can't always fight the tide or the current, we might use the current to get to a different place. 'Who can command circumstances?' Byron asked. 'The most we can do is avail ourselves of them.'

6

HOW TO HOPE

....

I should like to hope – but – but – always a *But*.
(Byron, letter to Teresa Guiccioli, 11 June 1819)

The question of what we might reasonably hope for from poetry was associated in Byron's mind with the question of what we might hope for from life. Take the following entry from his journal:

Memoranda.
What is Poetry? – The feeling of a Former world and Future.

Thought second.
Why, at the very height of desire and human pleasure, – worldly, social, amorous, ambitious, or even avaricious, – does there mingle a certain sense of doubt and sorrow – a fear of what is to come – a doubt of what *is* – a retrospect to the past, leading to a prognostication of the future? (The best of Prophets of the future is the Past.) Why is this?

or these? – I know not, except that on a pinnacle
we are most susceptible of giddiness, and that we
never fear falling except from a precipice – the
higher, the more awful, and the more sublime; and,
therefore, I am not sure that Fear is not a pleas-
urable sensation; at least, *Hope* is; and *what Hope*
is there without a deep leaven of Fear? and what
sensation is so delightful as Hope? and, if it were
not for Hope, where would the Future be? – in hell
. . . as for the Past, *what* predominates in memory?
– *Hope baffled*. Ergo, in all human affairs, it is Hope
– Hope – Hope.

(Ravenna Journal, 28 January 1821)

From the many toings and froings in this passage, it
emerges that 'Hope – Hope – Hope' is both a delight
and a predicament, something we should aspire to,
yet perhaps also avoid. Byron often tries to get to the
bottom of the questions raised here. It seems that
we're all hoping for something (a free upgrade; a happy
marriage; a dessert that features cream), but how can
we avoid being baffled by hope? What should – and
what shouldn't – we allow hope to do for us?

Hope certainly has its uses. For those who are ill, for
example, Byron notes that 'despair of all recovery spoils
longevity':

'Tis very certain the desire of life
  Prolongs it; this is obvious to physicians,
When patients, neither plagued with friends nor wife,
  Survive through very desperate conditions,
Because they can still hope . . .

                              (*Don Juan*, 1819–24)

But elsewhere in *Don Juan* the poet notes that hope is a mixed blessing. When some sailors, having abandoned ship, are drifting in their longboat on a still ocean, we are told that:

They hoped the wind would rise, these foolish men!
  And carry them to shore; these hopes were fine

                              (*Don Juan*, 1819–24)

So hope is somehow both 'foolish' and 'fine'. The men then catch sight of a rainbow:

Our shipwrecked seamen thought it a good omen;
  It is as well to think so, now and then;
'Twas an old custom of the Greek and Roman,
  And may become of great advantage when
Folks are discouraged; and most surely no men
  Had greater need to nerve themselves again
Than these, and so this rainbow looked like hope,
Quite a celestial kaleidoscope.

                              (*Don Juan*, 1819–24)

Hope, it is implied, provides us with an image of a future in order to get us through the present. The critic Arthur Hallam once noted that 'rhyme has been said to contain in itself a constant appeal to Memory and Hope', by which he meant that, as a structure of recollection and expectation, rhyme appeals to our need to link up past and future into patterns of predictability. The pleasure of Byron's final clinching couplet – in which 'hope' looks forward to, and chimes neatly with, 'kaleidoscope' – is a version of the sailors' pleasure. Things are going to turn out OK in the end; the stanza did, after all.

That said, Byron is also a great lover of rhymes that don't quite portend order: 'You might as well want a Midnight *all stars* – as rhyme all perfect,' he observed. In this stanza, 'again' is not a perfect chime with 'when' and 'then'. The slight glitch is the poet's way of intimating that certain hopes – for rhymes as well as for futures – may be misguided. Of all the words that should be allowed to go astray here, it's fitting that it should be 'again'. 'Again' is the promise of the repeatable, the predictable, the safe. In Byron's world, promises are made to be broken.

There is always hope, so the saying goes. But not for many of these sailors, as it transpires. Byron can be scathing about the Hope Brigade, and he invites us to be wary of their insistent chirpiness.

Hope is nothing but a false delay . . . what is Hope?
Nothing but the paint on the face of Existence; the
least touch of truth rubs it off, and then we see what
a hollow-cheeked harlot we have got hold of.

(Letter to Thomas Moore, 28 October 1815)

If there is always hope, there are always lots of other
things too. What, then, can really be hoped for from
hope?

First, the case for the prosecution. Byron has sometimes been described as a pessimist, and in some
moods he puts the case as strongly as anyone. One
hero growls:

> . . . *let boys hope*:
> Of Hope I now know nothing but the name –
> And that's a sound which jars upon my heart.
>
> (*Werner*, 1822)

Young hopefuls are precisely that – young. So hope is
what we grow out of, and one mark of maturity is dis-
illusionment. In another poem, the poet again follows
Hope with a 'but':

> They say that Hope is happiness;
>   But genuine Love must prize the past,
> And memory wakes the thoughts that bless:
>   They rose the first – they set the last;

And all that Memory loves the most
    Was once our only Hope to be,
And all that Hope adored and lost
    Hath melted into Memory.

Alas! it is delusion all:
  The future cheats us from afar,
Nor can we be what we recall,
    Nor dare we think on what we are.
           ('They Say that Hope is Happiness', 1816)

So, to be hopeful is to remember that we've been here many times before. Hope is a strangely attenuated, self-lacerating form of déjà vu. We are being tormented by a past that never quite made it into the present, and one that is unlikely to be found in the future.

But Byron's last line – 'Nor dare we think on what we are' – doesn't just lament the difficulty of how we often find ourselves placed. It also asks readers to consider what we are trying to avoid when we indulge in hope. One problem with hope is that it is so intent on foreseeing things that it forgets to see. Never give up hope, people are often told. But what has hope given up on? Hope can be a way of not being present to what's available from the here and now. If we dare to think on – and dare to be – what we are, then the unexpected might happen:

What are the hopes of man? Old Egypt's King
    Cheops erected the first pyramid,
And largest, thinking it was just the thing
    To keep his memory whole, and mummy hid;
But somebody or other rummaging,
    Burglariously broke his coffin's lid.
Let not a monument give you or me hopes,
Since not a pinch of dust remains of Cheops.

But I being fond of true philosophy
    Say very often to myself, 'Alas!
All things that have been born were born to die,
    And flesh (which Death mows down to hay) is grass.
You've passed your youth not so unpleasantly,
    And if you had it o'er again, 'twould pass;
So thank your stars that matters are no worse,
And read your Bible, sir, and mind your purse.'

                                    (*Don Juan*, 1819–24)

This time, the 'But' which follows talk of hope is not so crestfallen. The lines counsel us to lower our expectations so that we might heighten our receptiveness to how much has already been granted. As Byron's beloved Horace put it: 'The less I want, the more I seem to have.' In addition, the evident pleasure with which the lines have been composed also helps to offset the difficulties they describe. It's pleasing to be reminded that we have a word like 'burglariously' in the language (it delightfully teases out something glorious from within 'burglary'). Just rolling the word around your mouth makes loss sound like gain – a truly stolen pleasure.

While Byron's lines themselves are describing hopeless situations, the *sound* of the lines is often anything but disconsolate:

> Oh, there's not a joy the world can give like that it
>   takes away,
> When the glow of early youth declines in beauty's
>   dull decay;
> 'Tis not upon the cheek of youth the blush that
>   fades so fast,
> But the tender bloom of heart is gone ere youth
>   itself be past.
>
> ('Stanzas for Music', 1815)

G. K. Chesterton said that a recitation of these lines 'is the answer to the whole pessimism of Byron', and it's true that something curious happens if you read the stanza aloud: it makes you want to tap your feet. Byron's lines sing even when – *especially* when – all reasons for singing seem to have passed away. 'There is a very life in our despair,' he wrote on another occasion. This is one of the lessons of his poetry: loss of hope might provide us with an excuse to turn to a different kind of life or tune. Freed from expectancy, and freed from too clear a sense of what we thought we wanted, we are free to enjoy our loss of bearings, just as Childe Harold did:

> Self-exiled Harold wanders forth again,
> With nought of hope left, but with less of gloom.
> (*Childe Harold's Pilgrimage*, 1812–18)

'Comfort must not be expected by folks that go a pleasuring,' Byron wrote. He's saying that it's advisable not to set our expectations too high, but he's also hinting that there may be better things to be aiming for than comfort. Hope is teleological, and Byron is sceptical about appeals to endgames. 'It is odd,' he confessed. 'I never set myself seriously to wishing without attaining it – and repenting.' In the Ravenna Journal, just after his cogitations on 'Hope – Hope – Hope', he added: 'I allow sixteen minutes, though I never counted them, to any given or supposed possession.' So folks that go 'a pleasuring' (*all* of us, on a good day) should understand that hope may sometimes be a way of coping with a fear of the future by obsessing about it. In this incarnation, hope is really a terror of uncertainty. Byron invites us to wonder what we are missing out on if we miss out on uncertainty.

Hope can be a method for closing off the future, for refusing to let it just happen, to let it have its way with us. So the question becomes: Can we look forward to the future without generating too clear a picture of what it should look like? Can we learn, as the poet W. H. Auden put it, 'to approach the Future as a friend', without an 'embarrassing over-familiar gesture'? Byron offers models of this accommodation with the unknown when he thinks about the chances of an afterlife. Alluding to his club foot, he wrote to his friend Francis Hodgson:

> And our carcases, which are to rise again, are they worth raising? I hope, if mine is, that I shall have a better pair of legs than I have moved on these two-and-twenty years, or I shall be sadly behind in the squeeze into Paradise.
>
> (Letter to Francis Hodgson, 13 September 1811)

This wry smile at the limits of what even Paradise may be able to offer us is meant as a warning about what one can reasonably hope for from any future. Yet the smile itself is a consolation, and Byron could be severe with those who only hoped for the worst. He was not a supporter of King George III, for example, but then he was not keen on those who believed in the doctrine of eternal damnation that would see the tyrant punished for his sins:

> 'God save the king!' It is a large economy
>   In God to save the like; but if he will

Be saving, all the better; for not one am I
   Of those who think damnation better still: –
I hardly know too if not quite alone am I
   In this small hope of bettering future ill
By circumscribing, with some slight restriction,
The eternity of hell's hot jurisdiction.

(The Vision of Judgment, 1822)

'I know one may be damned / For hoping no one else may e'er be so,' the poet confesses later, but he hopes none the less – and he encourages us to follow his lead. In some guises, hope can be a way of being generous.

Two poets who owe a great debt to Byron help to show what he finally teaches us about hope. Giacomo Leopardi observes:

Man always desires and hopes for something he cannot understand . . . No human desires and hopes . . . are ever absolutely clear and distinct and precise, but always contain an idea of confusion, always refer to an object which is conceived confusedly. And for that reason and no other, hope is better than pleasure, because it contains that indefiniteness which reality cannot contain.

(Zibaldone, 1817–32, translated by
J. G. Nichols, in Canti, 2007)

From this perspective, the highest form of hope we could have would be to hope without trying to work out what we are hoping for. Indeed, the last time the word 'hope' appears in *Don Juan*, it is described as 'unbounded hope'. Another admirer of Byron, Charles Baudelaire, was pursuing a similar avenue of enquiry when he wrote: 'Only our hope is inexhaustible.' This kind of hope can be a salve, provided that we learn not to think of it as a salvation. Byron was adamant that 'when a man talks of system, his case is hopeless'. At its worst, hope can be a kind of system; at its best, it's a commitment to whatever in us cannot be exhausted or bounded or contained.

Byron once observed: 'Imagination resembles hope.' Resembles it, I think, because it entertains something without needing to finalize it. Mulling over his difficult circumstances, the poet rounded off one letter by saying: 'In the mean time I hope & laugh.' This might imply that he's laughing at the persistence of his own hope, or that his hope is somehow like his laughter. Or both: hope would then become a kind of pleasure as well as something to keep an eye on. This strikes the right note – at once sanguine and clear-sighted. It's a note that Byron hopes will strike a chord in us.

7

HOW TO SAY
GOODBYE

....

Nothing so difficult as a beginning
In poesy, unless perhaps the end
(Byron, *Don Juan*, 1819–24)

We are well versed in saying goodbye – to friends,
loved ones, homes, jobs – but endings often still feel
difficult. Best to plan ahead, Byron suggests, because:
'All must end in that wild word – farewell.' His life was
one long string of farewells – to his lovers, his wife
and his country. The first words spoken by his two
most celebrated characters – Childe Harold and Don
Juan – speak volumes; the former introduces himself
by crying 'Adieu', and the latter opens with 'Farewell'.
Like these men, Byron is an inveterate leave-taker, a
connoisseur of closure, forever searching for ways
to say goodbye. Retracing the steps of that search
presents us with some tricky questions: Why is it so
hard to say goodbye? Are there good and bad ways of
doing it? How can we reconcile ourselves to the need
for farewells?

'Adieu.' 'Farewell.' When Byron's heroes said this they were saying goodbye to their native shores, and the poet's most infamous goodbye was his departure from his own homeland in 1816. Rumours were being spread that he'd had homosexual liaisons, that he'd had sexual relations with his half-sister, and that he'd sodomized his wife. 'If what was whispered and muttered and murmured was true,' Byron commented, 'I was unfit for England, – if false – England was unfit for me.' Looking back on his distress a few years later, the poet admitted: 'I should have blown my brains out, but for the recollection that it would have given pleasure to my mother-in-law.'

One way to say goodbye is to move on. *Fast.* When Byron's boat reached Europe, he checked in to a hotel and – in his doctor's words – 'fell like a thunderbolt on the chambermaid'. But in his writing the poet isn't always in such a hurry, instead inviting us to think about what hurry might be trying to avoid. The day after Byron signed the agreement to separate from his wife, he wrote her the following lines:

> 'tis done – all words are idle –
> Words from me are vainer still;
> But the thoughts we cannot bridle
> Force their way without the will. –

Fare thee well! – thus disunited,
   Torn from every nearer tie,
Seared in heart, and lone, and blighted,
   More than this I scarce can die.

('Fare Thee Well!', 1816)

Byron knew that the relationship was over, and he knew that his feelings had changed too (he no longer loved her). So why should this kind of goodbye be felt as such an acute pain? Isn't the reference to dying here a mere affectation? Not necessarily. 'Every kind of parting has its stings,' wrote Byron in *Don Juan*. A reason for this had been suggested by one of the poet's favourite writers, Samuel Johnson (Byron referred to him as 'the noblest critical mind which our country has produced'). In his last *Idler* essay, Johnson wrote:

There are few things not purely evil, of which we can say, without some emotion of uneasiness, *this is the last*. Those who never could agree together, shed tears when mutual discontent has determined them to final separation; of a place which has been frequently visited, tho' without pleasure, the last look is taken with heaviness of heart . . . This secret horror of the last is inseparable from a thinking being whose life is limited, and to whom death is dreadful . . . when we have done any thing for the last time, we involuntarily reflect that a part of the days allotted to us is past, and that as more is past there is less remaining.

(Essay no. 103 of The Idler, 1760)

So, in addition to fears that often afflict people when saying goodbye ('Am I doing the right thing?') or when somebody is saying goodbye to them ('How can you be ending it like this?'), another disturbing thought may hover in the background. A farewell is a reminder that the clock is ticking. While we are running out on our pasts, time is running out on us.

Byron pondered the unexpected lessons that some goodbyes can provide when he adapted his own departure from his wife and country into fictional form in *Don Juan*:

Juan embarked, the ship got under way,
    The wind was fair, the water passing rough.
A devil of a sea rolls in that bay,
    As I, who've crossed it oft, know well enough.
And, standing upon deck, the dashing spray
    Flies in one's face, and makes it weather-tough.
And there he stood to take, and take again,
His first, perhaps his last, farewell of Spain.

I can't but say it is an awkward sight
    To see one's native land receding through
The growing waters; it unmans one quite,
    Especially when life is rather new.
I recollect Great Britain's coast looks white,
    But almost every other country's blue,
When gazing on them, mystified by distance,
We enter on our nautical existence . . .

Don Juan stood, and, gazing from the stern,
    Beheld his native Spain receding far:
First partings form a lesson hard to learn,
    Even nations feel this when they go to war;
There is a sort of unexprest concern,
    A kind of shock that sets one's heart ajar:
At leaving even the most unpleasant people
And places, one keeps looking at the steeple.

                        (*Don Juan*, 1819–24)

Partings do indeed 'form a lesson hard to learn'. They may clarify just how much we've taken for granted, revealing our 'unexprest concern' for the very thing that we are retreating from. A goodbye can suddenly make us feel strange to ourselves. Life feels 'rather new' in a rather unnerving way.

Perhaps, then, instead of rushing goodbyes, something might be gained from prolonging them – or rethinking them. In his letters, Byron often postpones endings by adding a P. S. (One postscript begins: 'P. S. – *Always* P. S.') His poems also present readers with a world in which everything is saying farewell luxuriously. Even the sun takes its time:

> Slow sinks, more lovely ere his race be run,
> Along Morea's hills the setting sun . . .
> The god of gladness sheds his parting smile;
> O'er his own regions lingering, loves to shine . . .
> Not yet – not yet – Sol pauses on the hill –
> The precious hour of parting lingers still
> (The Corsair, 1814)

The last stanza of *Childe Harold's Pilgrimage* begins:

> Farewell! a word that must be, and hath been –
> A sound which makes us linger.
> (Childe Harold's Pilgrimage, 1812–18)

Byron is the master of The Long Goodbye. For him, a good leave-taking involves a gradual lingering. His image of the setting sun here contains a further hint: a farewell is not quite the ending it pretends to be, because the sun will rise again tomorrow. Any particular end we face is not quite The End.

By cultivating this outlook on farewells, we might avoid the temptation to say goodbye too quickly. Those who try to abandon or bury their past – rather than to understand or acknowledge it – may, paradoxically, put themselves in more danger of being haunted by it. Byron encourages readers to cherish farewells that make space for residual – even regretful – feelings. One of his most beautiful poems says goodbye with grace:

So, we'll go no more a roving
  So late into the night,
Though the heart be still as loving,
  And the moon be still as bright.

For the sword outwears its sheath,
  And the soul wears out the breast,
And the heart must pause to breathe,
  And love itself have rest.

Though the night was made for loving,
  And the day returns too soon,
Yet we'll go no more a roving
  By the light of the moon.
                    ('So, we'll go no more a roving', 1817)

The poem allows for regret without allowing itself to be engulfed by regret, and in doing so it stands up to the fear of farewells. We may be afraid of goodbyes because we have cultivated a clear sense of what life is meant to have in store for us (so that saying goodbye is frightening because it launches us into a less predictable future); or because we're tied to the idea that longevity somehow equals success (people commonly refer, for example, to relationships that end as 'failed' relationships). Byron is wary of both ideas. Not to say goodbye can be to avoid and to diminish your future by sticking to a carefully orchestrated script – and to pretend to yourself that the script was forced on you, rather than made by you. Besides, all good things come to an end, and knowing when they *are* at an end is one way of not damaging their value.

'So, we'll go no more a roving' also hints at another truth about well-wrought goodbyes. Byron gives us an image of someone who is not so much putting the past behind them, as putting it *beside* them. Something is done, but not quite done *with*, because the poem senses that we can't be sure whether, or when, a relationship is really over. We can know that we are no longer seeing someone, but we can't know that they are no longer having an effect on us. We may 'go no more a roving', but who knows what continues to roam in the recesses of the mind and heart?

Byron wrote 'So, we'll go no more a roving' in Venice towards the end of the carnival in 1817. This is suggestive, because the carnival offers itself to readers as a valuable lesson in leave-taking. *Carne vale* means 'farewell to meat', as the poet later acknowledged when thinking about how the Venetians handled the art of departure:

'Tis known, at least it should be, that throughout
    All countries of the Catholic persuasion,
Some weeks before Shrove Tuesday comes about,
    The people take their fill of recreation,
And buy repentance, ere they grow devout,
    However high their rank, or low their station,
With fiddling, feast, dancing, drinking, masquing,
And other things which may be had for asking . . .

This feast is named the Carnival, which being
    Interpreted, implies 'farewell to flesh:'
So called, because the name and thing agreeing,
    Through Lent they live on fish both salt and fresh.
But why they usher Lent with so much glee in,
    Is more than I can tell, although I guess
'Tis as we take a glass with friends at parting,
In the stage-coach or packet, just at starting.

(Beppo, 1818)

What is celebrated here is the wisdom of saying goodbye with gusto. It's as though indulgence now is a means of smuggling a little bit of the present with you into a very different future. *One for the road*, as they say. The carnival turns parting into partying, and it does so to remind us that an ending can be reconceived as a form of 'starting'. Closure may be another word for adventure.

Byron finally teaches readers to face – and even to relish – goodbyes through the way he says goodbye to us. *Beppo* ends like this:

> My pen is at the bottom of a page,
>   Which being finished, here the story ends;
> 'Tis to be wished it had been sooner done,
> But stories somehow lengthen when begun.
>
> *(Beppo*, 1818)

He didn't just make this up – the manuscript shows that the poet really had arrived at the bottom of the page. But the larger implication is that, given half the chance, or given another bit of paper, the story might go on. The poet is intimating that his poem – like our lives – resembles the structure of a carnival itself: a pleasurably lengthened goodbye, one that keeps hinting at something to be continued. Essayist and psychotherapist Adam Phillips has suggested that 'when we finish a book – if it is a good one – it will not have ended. And neither will we. We can at least read to no foreseeable end.' There's no telling where a good book's effects on us might end. Byron was a great believer in how this conception of reading might be a helpful model for the art of living – not least because it helps us to face our futures with appetite rather than apprehension.

At the end of the first canto of *Don Juan*, Byron says goodbye again:

> But for the present, gentle readers, and
>   Still gentler purchaser, the bard – that's I –
> Must with permission shake you by the hand,
>   And so your humble servant, and good-bye.
> We meet again, if we should understand
>   Each other; and if not, I shall not try
> Your patience further than by this short sample.
> 'Twere well if others followed my example.
>
> *(Don Juan,* 1819–24)

Readers can follow the poet's example here by cultivating in themselves a sense of an ending that leaves
something open-ended. We need to start seeing and
accepting our goodbyes not as last words, nor as wholly
new beginnings, but as ambiguous transitions, or as
indeterminate preludes to something else. At the end
of the second canto the poet says goodbye once more
as he takes leave of the young lovers, Juan and Haidee:

> In the meantime, without proceeding more
>   In this anatomy, I've finished now
> Two hundred and odd stanzas as before,
>   That being about the number I'll allow
> Each canto of the twelve, or twenty-four;
>   And, laying down my pen, I make my bow,
> Leaving Don Juan and Haidee to plead
> For them and theirs with all who deign to read.
>
> *(Don Juan,* 1819–24)

'I've finished now': it initially sounds as if things are done and dusted, but as we read on we discover that what Byron really means is that 'I've finished ... for now'. There are more cantos to come (there are always more stories to be told), and Byron never did finish the poem. He did something better; he kept adding to it. One of the poet's most enduring life lessons is captured in his willingness to leave not just Don Juan and Haidee, but also his readers, in an eternally suspended present tense. In books as in life, saying goodbye is another way of saying that you are leaving yourself and others with unfinished business, and with something to play for.

CODA:
WHAT BYRON MEANS TO ME

....

I do detest everything which is not perfectly mutual.
(Byron, letter to Lady Melbourne, 21 October 1813)

I first encountered Byron at university. There were no lectures on him, but an enthusiastic tutor recommended that I dive into *Don Juan*. The first thing I warmed to was the poet's assumption that he and I had been on intimate terms for quite some time. An early reviewer said that, reading Byron's verses: 'They are not felt, while we read, as declarations published to the world, – but almost as secrets whispered to chosen ears . . . we feel as if chosen out from a crowd of lovers.' This rang true; Byron is a great payer of compliments. It felt as though the poet had imagined me into existence as a reader for whom not everything needed to be spelled out. When thinking how much he should divulge, he wrote:

> we had better not
> Be too minute; an outline is the best —
> A lively reader's fancy does the rest.
> (*Don Juan*, 1819–24)

I liked being thought of as lively. Byron's point was similar to Laurence Sterne's in *Tristram Shandy*, a novel he greatly admired:

> Writing, when properly managed, (as you may be sure I think mine is) is but a different name for conversation . . . no one, who knows what he is about in good company, would venture to talk all . . . The truest respect which you can pay to the reader's understanding, is to halve this matter amicably, and leave him something to imagine, in his turn, as well as yourself.
>
> (Laurence Sterne, *Tristram Shandy*, 1759–67)

Byron was the writer who first showed me just how much imagination goes into understanding.

Later, the poet suggested: "Tis not enough to spell or even to read / To constitute a reader.' I took this to mean that I needed to convert the seclusion of reading and the silence of the printed page into forms of ongoing exchange. Byron himself confessed that, even when writing poetry:

> I rattle on exactly as I'd talk
> With any body in a ride or walk.
>
> (*Don Juan*, 1819–24)

I wanted to rattle on too, to quote him to others, and to have him quoted back. He praised the poet Thomas

Campbell by saying that 'he deepens our social interest in existence', and this was Byron's own effect upon me.

> I'm fond of fire and crickets and all that,
> A lobster salad and champagne and chat.
>
> (*Don Juan*, 1819–24)

Let's chat, his poems said.

I hope that my sense of what can be learned from Byron is not an isolated feeling; on several occasions in this book I have written 'we' rather than 'I'. The poet was sometimes sceptical about this rhetorical ploy; in one essay, he wrote: 'I – that is We – (for the anonymous – like Sovereigns multiply the Egotism into the plural number)'. Certainly, the royal We may take liberties, and Byron often laughed at those who presumed too much. His rejoinder to somebody who used the phrase 'as the reader will see' was: 'I am a reader – a "gentle reader" – and I see nothing of the kind.' Yet this leap from 'I' to 'we', or from writer to reader, is a risk he thought worth taking, and his poetry is founded on an appeal to shared thoughts and experience:

> let us ponder boldly – 'tis a base
> Abandonment of reason to resign
> Our right of thought – our last and only place
> Of refuge; this, at least, shall still be mine.
>
> (*Childe Harold's Pilgrimage*, 1812–18)

This book is an invitation to continue pondering boldly with the poet. His 'thought' and 'refuge' can be ours, for, as the poet William Henley noted: 'Byron's personality was many-sided enough to make his egoism representative.'

When I first read Byron as a student, I thought that he was a great poet of reason, and of the reasonable. I continued to think that, but what I thought also got tangled up with what I felt. (Besides, as Byron points out in *Don Juan*: 'Man, being reasonable, must get drunk.') I went to study as a postgraduate student in Bologna – learning Italian, reading more Byron, drinking it all in and falling in love while the sound of his poetry played in the background. 'With all its sinful doings, I must say, / That Italy's a pleasant place to me,' he confesses in *Beppo*:

I love the language, that soft bastard Latin,
    Which melts like kisses from a female mouth,
And sounds as if it should be writ on satin,
    With syllables which breathe of the sweet
    South . . .

I like the women too (forgive my folly),
    From the rich peasant cheek of ruddy bronze,
And large black eyes that flash on you a volley
    Of rays that say a thousand things at once
                                    (*Beppo*, 1818)

Italy was a good place to learn what mouths, syllables and eyes might do when given licence to roam. When I returned to England, I went on reading, thinking and writing about Byron. Like the large black eyes he was so drawn to, his words still seem to say a thousand things at once. Nowadays I teach Byron, which is just another way of saying that I continue to take lessons in him.

For Byron and for those who read him, to learn is to yearn. The poet very rarely gives clear-cut answers or prescriptions ('do a, b, or c to get a better life'). He tends towards provocation, not precept; 'I am quick-silver, and say nothing positively,' he explained. 'I deny nothing, but doubt everything.' Yet Byron does remain committed to trying to imagine what a good life might look and feel like, a life he described as 'at once adven-turous and contemplative'. It's a life embodied in the life of his writing, and that writing is anyone's adventure.

But now to have absorbed the lesson, to have recovered from the shock of not being able to remember it, to again be setting out from the beginning – is this not something good to you?

John Ashbery, 'The System', in *Three Poems* (1989)

HOMEWORK

1
HOW TO BECOME YOURSELF
....

Charles Taylor's *The Sources of the Self* (1989) is a seminal exploration of many things a self might be. On the adventure of becoming yourself, see Christopher Bollas's *Being a Character: Psychoanalysis and Self Experience* (1993). Irving Goffman's *The Presentation of Self in Everyday Life* (1959) explores the ways we perform ourselves. Two other great meditations on selfhood are Carl Jung's *Memories, Dreams, Reflections* (1963), and *Roland Barthes by Roland Barthes*, translated by Richard Howard (2010).

2
HOW TO THINK WITH YOUR BODY
....

On how our language is steeped in our bodies, see George Lakoff and Mark Johnson's *Metaphors We Live By* (1991). Antonio Damasio's *The Feeling of What Happens: Body, Emotion and the Making of Consciousness* (2000) explores the neurobiology of feeling, thought and emotion. Mark Williams's *Mindfulness: A Practical*

Guide to Finding Peace in a Frantic World (2011) provides insight into what your body can do for your mind. On why dance is for everyone, see *Napoleon Dynamite* (2004): http://www.youtube.com/watch?v=BiAwpYIkRmU.

3
HOW TO LAUGH

....

W. H. Auden's essays, 'Notes on the Comic' and '*Don Juan*', in *The Dyer's Hand* (1968) are full of good things. Norman Holland's book *Laughing* (1982) is engaging, as is Robert Provine's *Laughter: A Scientific Investigation* (2000). The film-documentary *The Aristocrats* (2005) is a darkly delightful meditation on what we need jokes to do for us, and Jimmy Carr and Lucy Greeves's *The Naked Jape: Uncovering the Hidden World of Jokes* (2006), is wise as well as witty. See also Ted Cohen's great little book, *Jokes: Philosophical Thoughts on Joking Matters* (1999).

4
HOW TO GO ASTRAY

....

Montaigne's *Essays*, translated by M. A. Screech (2003), are enduring guides to going astray as part of the art of living. See also Sarah Bakewell's *How to Live: a Life of Montaigne in one question and twenty attempts at an answer* (2011). Laurence Sterne's *The Life and Opinions of Tristram Shandy, Gentleman*, edited by Melvyn New (2003), shows what can be gained from digression. Henry David Thoreau's *Walden* and his *Journals 1837–1861*, edited by John Stilgoe (2009), tell of how one man got lost in order to get found, and Stanley Cavell ponders the wonderful mystery further in *The Senses of Walden* (1992). See also Rebecca Solnit's *A Field Guide to Getting Lost* (2006).

5
HOW TO GET WET

....

On the ways in which we can use water to think with, see Gaston Bachelard's *Water and Dreams*, translated by Edith Farrell (1999). William Empson's poem about alcohol, 'Bacchus', contains the following note in true Byronic spirit: 'Life involves maintaining oneself between contradictions that can't be solved by analysis . . . what strength or wisdom the drink gives comes through disturbing you.' For the most invigorating of soakings, try Alice Oswald's *Dart* (2002) and Roger Deakin's *Waterlog* (2000). Only tangentially related – but bracing nonetheless – is David Foster Wallace's speech, 'This is Water', given to Kenyon College's graduating class: http://www.youtube.com/watch?v=cZXljbi57Hg.

6
HOW TO HOPE
....

Byron's relationship with hopes of various kinds can be gleaned from his superb letters – see *Lord Byron: Selected Letters and Journals*, edited by Leslie Marchand (1982). Leopardi pushes hope to the limit in his *Canti*, translated by J. G. Nichols (2007). Spinoza has thought-provoking things to say about hope and fear in the *Ethics*, translated by Edwin Curley (2005). See also Richard Rorty's *Philosophy and Social Hope* (1999), and Adam Phillips's 'On the Value of Frustration' for the journal *World Picture*: http://www.worldpicturejournal.com/WP_3/Phillips.html.

7
HOW TO SAY GOODBYE
....

For a wry meditation on goodbyes, see the end of Woody Allen's *Annie Hall* (1977): http://www.youtube.com/watch?v=W-M3Q2zhGd4. Bob Dylan's *Blood on the Tracks* (1975) ponders bust-ups and break-ups, leave-takings and loneliness, among other things. On endings more generally, see Frank Kermode's study, *The Sense of an Ending* (1965). I mull over our need for endgames of various kinds in chapter 8 of *Comedy: A Very Short Introduction* (2012). On the art of loving and losing, see Elizabeth Bishop's poem, 'One Art'.

ACKNOWLEDGEMENTS

....

Many thanks to Jon Butler for suggesting that I write on Byron, and to Cindy Chan for helping the thing to take shape. I'm especially grateful to the book's first readers – Adam Phillips, Hugh Haughton and Rebecca Bevis – for ideas, conversation, and encouragement.